Restless
Messengers

Restless Messengers

POEMS BY

Norman Finkelstein

The University of Georgia Press

Athens and London

© 1992 by Norman Finkelstein
Published by the University of Georgia Press
Athens, Georgia 30602
All rights reserved
Designed by Betty Palmer McDaniel
Set in Trump Mediaeval
The paper in this book meets the guidelines for permanence and durability
of the Committee on Production Guidelines for Book Longevity of the
Council on Library Resources.

Printed in the United States of America

96 95 94 93 92   C   5 4 3 2 1

96 95 94 93 92   P   5 4 3 2 1

Library of Congress Cataloging in Publication Data

Finkelstein, Norman, 1954–
Restless messengers : poems / by Norman Finkelstein.
p.   cm.
ISBN 0-8203-1379-3 (alk. paper).
—ISBN 0-8203-1380-7 (pbk. : alk. paper)
I. Title.
PS3556.I484R47   1992
811'.54—dc20   91-12701
CIP

British Library Cataloging in Publication Data available

The publication of this book is supported by a grant
from the National Endowment for the Arts,
a federal agency.

He was clothed nearly all in white; not in silk, of course—he was in winter clothes like all the others—but the material he was wearing had the softness and dignity of silk. His face was clear and frank, his eyes larger than ordinary. His smile was unusually joyous; he drew his hand over his face as if to conceal the smile, but in vain. "Who are you?" asked K. "My name is Barnabas," he said; "I am a messenger."

—KAFKA,
The Castle

The author and publisher gratefully acknowledge the following publications in which poems in this volume first appeared, sometimes in a different form.

Ambergris: "The Master of Turning"
Denver Quarterly: "Moldavanka," "Sketch for a Portrait," "The Weary Pleasure Seekers"
Missouri Review: "From the Archives"
Salmagundi: "A Poem for the Little Shoemakers," "Braids," "A Poem for the Great Heresy," "Odradek," "Exile," "Job's Daughter's," "Mládi"
Shofar: "My Father's Yahrzeit," "Homage to Naftali Brandwine," "Friday Night in the Garden of Eden"
Talisman: "אֱמֶת," "from Four Impromptus"

The author wishes to extend special thanks to Robert Boyers, the editor of *Salmagundi,* for his early and continual support of the poetry in this volume.

Contents

Restless
Messengers

A Poem for the Little Shoemakers

The sunset opens against the horizon
      like a book in which are inscribed
the deeds of a thousand generations—
      and yet the pages are blank.
      Nothing but sentiment
            among the hosts of heaven,
      while here on earth
            the black smoke rises
      as the villages are consumed.

To be scattered among the nations
      and seek through codes of piety
to raise the sparks of creation,
      or to follow some leader
            into the maw of the abyss:
the choices are dashed on the rocks
      and the rocks are worn into dust.
There is nothing to be learned from patience
      except for the most minute of wonders:
            toadstools around the door
and moss growing softly in the rafters,
      a halo of clouds around the moon,
            stars when the moon is new.

And then to turn and worship the invisible,
      creation wrenched once more from a book,
      an alphabet of living forms.
      Why are we held back, oh Lord?
the cry rising from the corners of the world,
anxious to escape the workshops and kitchens,
      chipped plates, mismatched silverware,

love weaving itself into a carpet,
as wealth suddenly breeds and thrives,
an exile wrought in gold.

So lean into the past:
Somewhere is a house that is the navel of the world.
In winter the wolves come down out of the mountains,
and in spring the goats seek the higher pastures,
but the shoemaker sits at his bench forever
and the people walk back and forth upon the earth.
For this is merely the story of a passage
not from one land to another
nor from one world to the next,
but into the living structure of memory,
as that alone must suffice.
The books are submerged in a great repository
or consumed by braided flames;
the Throne of Justice is vacant
as it was always meant to be

—but the sun is warming the shoemaker's shed
and his hammer, striking the worn sole,
seems to make the sparks fly up into the light.

A Poem for Orphans

It is an illusion that we were ever alive,
Lived in the houses of mothers . . .
—WALLACE STEVENS

Stretching away from childhood in a gentle curve,
the grass was blue in the shadow of the spruce
   and the slanting beams of the setting sun
     grew ever more remote.
   Rubble on the face of the moon
   riding the milky blue of the sky:
my chilled limbs straggled across the lawn
   to be greeted by ministering hands.
There are so many poignant evaporations,
   as the solid house, the sturdy tree,
   the hammock cocoon of delightful rest
     come to a term and pass.
My dreams flee and I cannot tell
   if I wished them to linger or not.
On a midsummer night they may go out dancing,
   bare shoulders, lights by the cascades,
   a shadowy orchestra in the pavilion
     playing an old jazz tune.
Would they have brought me back to tidy streets,
   bakery storefronts, submerged fish markets
where the thud of the cleaver severed the spine?
Would they have opened on fields of choking goldenrod,
where the old horses breathed out leather and dung
   and the tall girls laughed at my timid skills?
I cannot consider the kisses in the mountains,
    kisses at the shore,
the quivering backs of my melancholy sisters,

3

gone from me now in indulgent regret.
Be comforted, children—your loss is your own;
you will carry it with you out of orphaned childhood,
you will be orphaned from your childhood,
notwithstanding your parents,
your lovers, children of your own.

Exile

One day you will walk (as I have walked)
in a place of utterly innocent dimensions,
      park or alley, basement or hill,
the impenetrable site of everyday rituals,
and come upon something you thought you had lost,
      extinct, consigned to that distant sphere
          of objects traded to oblivion.
          Seize it before it disappears:
it is the profane image of a forgotten love;
and though it has long since yielded to the material world,
          take it again to your heart.
But as your gaze is met by its presence,
          returned by its sentience,
the world slips further into itself.
Some greater dispersal is taking place
and even the melancholy of objects is gone.
          Vacant and moribund, the world
          ceases to even long for itself;
voices are silenced, words are unmade.

A wind is blowing through this well-ordered house:
      a window is opened, and then another;
      the letters are strewn across the desk;
      the pot boils over on the stove.
          Suddenly there is motion:
      the lovers slip into the bedroom,
      children chase a ball across the lawn
      as their mother sits down at the piano
      and their father talks to a friend.
      Who has not eaten at their table?
And how long has it been since you were asked to leave,

pursuing that same irrepressible breeze
that led you from bedroom to parlor to kitchen,
        sites of arrested remembrance?

        You think you will wander forever,
        for the house has been left in ruin
and further upheavals are always promised
by pundits, soothsayers and wicked messengers
        who turn up as if appointed
by the angel who covers your days.
So you dream of the pure revolutionary act,
anarchist miracle, popular uprising,
window opening upon the Messianic world
—"he will come, not on the last day,
        but on the very last"—
        bitterest joke of all.

        You cannot begin to refine this speech,
        collect the fallen scraps of history
and make a cloak to wear as you go out walking,
        thinking about your love.
        A song hovers above the trees,
settles in the branches, turns into a bird.

The Master of Turning

I have chosen to live in this little town,
away from the courts, away from the schools.
I watch the children play in the streets
and the old women make their way home from the market.
The sea is salt; birds faintly sing;
trouble darkens the roads and the cities,
broods in the skies above our heads.

Because I have grown to love simplicity,
people consider me simple.
Nor have I the wish to change their minds:
I cannot: my powers being such
that my words stand still and are gathered against the void
that opens before them at every instant
I am called upon to speak.
I was called upon to speak,
but another voice whispered against the will of my utterance:
"Come away; you will be misunderstood.
I will prepare a place where the wise do not go
and there you may speak and be silent."

So in the autumn, when the cold's false promises
revive us for a little while,
I distributed kisses and handshakes,
and my friends, seeming to be content,
allowed me to say goodbye.
Had I been misled?
Saints have been known to hide themselves away,
and I have read that there are thirty-six men
upon whom rests the fate of the world.
I love the old tales; their leisured music
is born out of poverty, so that they become an inheritance

—but I do not think there are any such men.
Their numbers are endlessly multiplied
and so they will continue
until the world recognizes the product of itself
in the mirror of its grand tabulations.

But a single man cannot contain multitudes
and Adam Kadmon sleeps on,
dreaming in circles that the future is the past.
Suppose time has stopped,
our errors damming that purposeful river,
so that in well watered gardens, lush and secluded,
poets sing and politicians plot strategies
in a moment of repose that endures forever.

And does the light that falls upon the trees there
fall through my window too?
It seems vain to think otherwise
—but the heart of the world, as it dwells in the parable,
cried out to me, so that I forgave myself
both my dreams and my misgivings
and went my way in peace.

And I came that day to the fountain
about which I have been forbidden to speak,
so that there are blanks in the writing
as if a divine censor had struck out the words,
leaving me with nothing but the etceteras of history,
while the apparatchiks chortled into their beer,
taking it all for a sign.
If I were to upbraid them, my most extravagant claims
would be fulfilled:

upon such conditions, soup cooks,
bread rises,
and stories remain to be told.

Hans My Hedgehog

I want to go back, out of the bad stories,
But there's always the possibility that the next one . . .
—JOHN ASHBERY

The forest world begins at the doorstep;
I have only to come out from behind the stove,
     pick up my bagpipes and be gone.
Father, let the cockerel be shod;
I will lead the herds away from here
     and never trouble you again.

What else could you have given me
as I shift in and out of your life?
I left the princess naked and torn
because the king too thought of nothing but himself.
     I prefer the austerity of hapless events,
my feckless life, into which I pour
     adventures, as into a sieve.

Astonishing lights in the deeps of the wood
     prove to be campfires
around which sprawl the same tired bands
     of brigands, who are easily fooled.
The gilded pleasures of the story itself
     suggest that I should surface,
forget the pearls and sunken treasures,
     however they color my dreams.

But I must still wait to cast off my skin,
     throw it into the fire of symbols

that consumes the fiction of the old self,
leaving a white narrative in its place.
    Only then will Hans be content
and the urchin who made himself a hero
will rest, come what may.

New Lamps for Old

She sent down her maid,
and smiling, watched from the balcony.
The children had gathered around him,
and he let her pick from the basket:
it was nothing but rank folly,
and the marketplace rang with laughter.

But he almost got his revenge,
this wily, hardworking master of mischief,
pitted against a lazy boy
whose luck always held out.
There was a picture of the cave with bowls of gems,
diamonds and rubies, emeralds and sapphires,
strange fruit like the bags of marbles
sold in the museum shop.

I was the boy who had seen the princess
and sent her sweet love like sparks of colored glass,
cat's-eyes twinkling in the corner of the sofa
or beneath the piano on the living room rug.
Watch out or he'll spirit it all away!
the palace transported from China to Africa,
where she'll live out her days in despair.

I am not the genie of the lamp,
but only the genie of the ring.
I can take you there but cannot perform the rescue,
which depends solely on your cunning and devotion
to the lady and the throne.

It always comes down to chicanery and murder,
as through the curving arches, curving swords
painted by some traveller on his way through Morocco
are seen to flash and disappear
in the glare of the afternoon sun.
It made my head spin when, closing the book,
I went off gratefully to bed.

But what remains remains for a long time,
repeating itself endlessly in a haze of color,
the first sight of jewels in hidden places
and the adventures which always ensue.

The Piper at the Gates of Dawn

Lest the awful remembrance should remain and grow,
and overshadow mirth and pleasure, and the great
haunting melody should spoil all the after-lives of
little animals helped out of difficulties, in order that
they should be happy and lighthearted as before.
—KENNETH GRAHAME,
The Wind in the Willows

We little animals living by the river banks,
burrowers and swimmers by sandy shores:
was there ever a time when the bird's song,
giving way in evening to the flight of the bat,
failed to presage a momentary chill,
          even on summer days?

The warm folds of forgetfulness
          are meant to be comforting:
but how soon they cease to soothe us,
          haunted as we shall always be
by the absent music, the departing hand.

          Yes, we are full of Panic life;
it flows deep within us, nor are we out of touch
          with the powers that watch us survive.
          But the banks get crowded
          or fall away steeply,
and someone is always getting trampled or drowned.
It's then that the music, seeming to have gone,
glides through the reeds on its sinuous way.

          And though we are not its destination,
neither are we bystanders happening along the path.

We are neither forgotten nor remembered,
       but somehow have been included:
we know that for us it always comes to good
       and that must be enough.

Moldavanka

With raspberry waistcoats, lemon boots,
      their chocolate coattails streaming out behind,
they rush down alleyways at steamy midnight;
      or in grand coaches, off to see their whores,
          parade before impassive crones.

This is Odessa, this is how it's done:
      the page wears spectacles, peers into my own.
Sweetness is strength, pleasure is violence—
      do not look away.
      There's more to be learned on the waterfront
          than in any rabbi's study;
          for the Torah is a fountain,
      but does it flow like Bessarabian wine?

Drink and forget the ensuing generations,
      their escapes, apartments, small lawns of home.
The pious gangster is soothed by illusions,
      but the revolutionary intellect bursts into flame,
      rides with Cossacks to visit heathen priests
          where the moon is a cheap earring
      and the students shiver by the stove.

      A roll with onions, a shot of rum—
anything to stop these speeches in my head!
      When Grandfather was a little boy,
      the teacher would fall asleep in class,
      so they glued his beard to the desk.
      But I would have paid attention,
      waiting respectfully until he awoke
          so the lesson might go on.

For I have chained myself to the Gemara,
though the texts have long since rotted away,
till all that's left is the afterlife of the spirit,
the matter of the poem.

In the thieves' quarter everything is stolen;
bootleggers and smugglers bring the news
with olive oil, paprika and sardines.
Do not trust them—the messenger
has been waylaid somewhere outside of town.
It's Friday night, but he'll transgress the Sabbath
in order to bring you the Word.

Summer

He took one road
and she took another,
but they promised to meet
between the Black Fast and the White.

And that is how it goes
here at the Blue Hedgehog.

Didn't they travel
into some far country,
only to return
as night was falling?

A pitcher of cream
and a bowl of raspberries
set out on the table.

How abruptly the voices
take it all away.

Hair and limbs
and paper moonlight.
The breeze along the spine,
impossibly remote.

Sequestered,
lips lifted,
they gave themselves away.

And that is how it goes
here at the Blue Hedgehog.

He was beside himself;
she wondered about regret.
The road near the town
glowed in the lamplight.

How abruptly the voices
take it all away.

The Weary Pleasure Seekers

it is the end of any season
—JOHN ASHBERY

Godfather Death, we are not quite ready.
One by one, the trees fall asleep,
but the fruit is still piled high on the tables
and there is wine left in the glasses
though some has spilled on the ground.
The children are crying for one more trip
down the water slide, or one more ride
on the wheel that takes them up past the sun,
forever pointed west.

Even in moments of contentment,
knowledge troubles the painstaking calm.
Exhausted faces try to smile
as the cat peers at the fattening squirrel
and makes her way off the porch.
Go on tasting the afternoon:
apples, honey cake and tea.
Once I had friends who made love in this weather,
the air cooling their heated bodies,
but that was long ago.

Such turns are inevitable:
only let them be graceful,
viewed from a distance that is never as far as it seems.
Time turns continually into space,
as if it were meant to be nothing but a stage
for images: another minor scandal
for those inclined to philosophize on their orchard walks.

Nor is it easy to bear the shame
of random leisure, momentarily preserving
        discrete sensations, isolated joys.
Well-appointed houses give themselves for a while,
receding into the stuff of novels too long to read.
No wonder the children's books litter the carpet,
lying open to pictures of lawns and gardens
with tiny figures hiding or running away.
These friendly, lonely ones—is it with joy or fear
        that they call to you,
        Godfather Death?

Les Adieux

As if you could flee
    like some nobleman's family
        from invading troops—

The cannon of the conqueror
    heard just outside the city
        as the coach pulls away—

As if you could see
    beyond the horizon of pleasure,
        of casual gratification,
            arrested in time—

The avenues are blockaded
    to the probing of consciousness
        as music sweeps you forward—

Or are you riding backwards,
    the Absolute on horseback,
        to dwell among philosophers
            in the grand hotel—

At the edge of the abyss
    where the allegories are indecipherable,
        the programs are abandoned—

Music turns in upon itself,
    turns its back on necessity,
        loses its urgency—

You are moving through a landscape
        that once seemed beyond reach
            but has been finally rendered
                on a paper backdrop—

The moon rises
        as if something were beginning,
            the chastened lyricism
                of a thousand farewells—

Again you have set out
        after promising to return,
            as if devotion were a sonata
                seeking its end—

The capital has fallen,
        the people are in mourning,
            but the piano plays on,
                progressing in great circles—

The chamber empties,
        the circles widen,
            the boundaries dissolve—

Schubertiade

but Schubert is gone,
the genius of his melody
has passt, and all the lovely marrd sentiment
—ROBERT DUNCAN

Wood panelling to honor my father;
the "baby grand" my mother loved;
and for me, a woman whose floating voice
rises above the lamps and chairs
till it encircles the hall and settles among us
as light, shadow and light.

And the arms of night
are words on a page, notes in air,
the lyric sheen of neglected heights
seen from a still unmeasured distance—
Love enhances us
and as the strings stir,
voice thrills us
or hammers strike strings,
the movement is such
that we in our restlessness
sing.

To whom?
Of what did I dream when music woke me,
the cold hand of medieval death
hanging above the lyric gestures
like the lost original
of some antique pageant?
Shake off the dust!

When I was cautioned to avoid
too many questions or commands,
I did not dream my teacher
was questioning, commanding,
        going to meet death
before the lesson was done.

Before the sweet, nostalgic moments
        coalesce, evaporate,
leave us with the stridency
        of quotidian joys,
listen: the *unheimlich* is rare,
we fail to recognize its approach,
for homelessness has become
        our native element.
And I am apart from you,
cannot be borne closer;
my inventiveness fails me,
        stutters, dies.
Only this: through a haze of words,
        street sounds, demands,
time opens a space in happenstance
for the sense to filter through.

Nor is it the lack of a center:
        there is no center
        or it is everywhere,
so we banished mathematical false rigors
in favor of a leisure we could not afford.
                We:
company too, the greatest leisure,
more pleasurable for its fictitiousness.
We imagine ourselves a company,
the I having proven a failure,
                necessary,

but somehow surpassed.
All good things
eradicate themselves
in order to realize their worth.
The silence after the line suggests
its germination in thought;
silent thought breaking itself
on speech,
privacies inevitably gone.

So we return to a room
where the thinker reads,
writes in a book,
plays the piano
or, seeking love,
visits gardens, bedrooms, nurseries, kitchens,
satisfactions impossible to deny.
Give love back to them all,
replenish them,
not out of any abstract responsibility
but as the lovers suddenly find themselves
entangled—well!
this is the lure and reward.

And in creation the process turns again,
seeking resolution.
They are coming to an end.
Soon we will be given back to ourselves,
each private universe sold back to us,
returned: used goods.
Linger a moment here.
I think of them all giving back to death
his due, but stealing a little,
or keeping what is rightfully theirs.
I will keep it for you,

nurture it,
be the parents of its ingathering,
mother and father rescued
as the child fades into sleep.
And its outpouring recurs,
eminently believable,
apart,
a part,
until the voice is still.

A Poem for Storytellers

A handful of stories is all one has to offer
     even in seeking to remake the world.
If the seventh beggar, the legless one,
     could tell his tale and dance at the wedding,
      all would be restored.
But the message is lost in the act of transmission
     and the wisdom has long since decayed.
The beautiful maiden leaves the king's court
     and goes off on her own.
     So the tale begins
    but it never finds its ending,
as the impulse is finally dissipated
    and lost in windy silence.

Pieces for Children

Somewhere among the calendar's pages
is a window which opens upon an inviolable dimension,
a space like a house hidden among clichés
of the temperate seasons of lost youth.

Long after the children have taken rooms in the city
and piano notes like snow have drifted into heaps,
the years' accumulation played out of tedium,
vague longing for someone who never arrived,
the eyes of lovers, fireflies at dusk,
remain an ephemeral monument
to an unobtainable past.

Whoever lays claim to such ardent fabrications
must understand how the superfluous ones go on their way,
forever taking stock of private ceremonies
while the ruthless analysis proceeds apace
and the wind laughs in the corn.

From the Archives

... devout believers are safeguarded in a high degree
against the risks of certain neurotic illnesses; their
acceptance of the universal neuroses spares them the
task of constructing a personal one.

—FREUD,

The Future of an Illusion

As inevitable as the china closet
　　　　in the dining room,
faith, appraised by the antique dealers of Vienna,
　　Berlin, Prague, Warsaw and Paris,
　　San Francisco by way of New York,
hardly stands a chance of maintaining its value
in a marketplace flooded with cheaper commodities.

　　That's Father there on the whatnot:
once upon a time he was a book in the library;
　　　then he became a space on the shelf.
　　For the individual and the universal
　　　　are indistinguishable,
　　neurosis having gone out of style.

　　One senses a massive evasion,
but wherever one turns, the signs of honesty
swing like shingles above shopkeepers' doors.
　　The pale satisfactions of science
　　　are no illusion, but open on a world
cured of devotion by interminable analysis.
What young man would not stand aside and weep
for the wayward cleric, the lost sea captain,
and the parlormaid in the hands of the clever seducer?

So traffic in dreams
becomes an exercise in nostalgia,
as the table is set for the annual dinner,
the group portrait to be found in a textbook
a hundred years hence.

A Poem for the Erl King

Only you, it seems, can supplant the father
riding into the night, the grown-up future
where the man is comforted in comforting the child.
Only you, with your mother and daughters,
gray willows, shreds of mist,
can steal into childhood so convincingly
that the tenacious grip is broken
and the spirit of youth glides away.

Before all else you put the innocent form
which you take by force when persuasion won't suffice.
Death's younger brother, you have a different wisdom;
you know all the family secrets,
the ways in which severity gives in to love.

Gar schöne Spiele spiel ich mit dir;
Fort! Da! so the game is played
and who knows if we want to win or lose?
Even you, with your promises,
your flowers and dances,
can barely compensate for the primal loss,
the beloved object
which substitutes for a state we can never know.

That is your kingdom, lord of shadows:
the notes ripple as the century tilts
toward the old man in the study of Berggasse 19
and the children are taken from all the fathers' arms.

Brahms: Waltz (Op. 39, No. 15)

As the departing soul looks down upon the earth
and its gaze sweeps the grass, takes in the house
where time still lingers among tasks left undone:

so the hands hover once more over the keys,
and the melody, full of outworn desire,
repeats itself before it is extinguished.

Barnabas

after reading The Castle

You dress in white, as if to disappear against the snow.
But your youth cuts a figure against all backgrounds;
your smile radiates outward; and your foolish hopes
illuminate even the dimmest rooms you must visit.

You would wonder at me, but I am afraid to address you:
what you are sets you both before me and behind,
and you are in no way the figure I can now expect
to approach me: I must seduce you, messenger, virgin.

Odradek

Amidst no more cares than those of any other man,
    he pauses anywhere, perhaps on the stairs
or in the lobby, its fallen grandeur of tiles,
    dark wood and beveled glass abandoned
    to the sullen magistrates of dust.
    Beset by fear, he is hardly surprised
at the stirring in the corner, the whimper of a sigh,
and drags himself forward, limping into the light
    cast by a dim, unbroken lamp.

In the old stories, such doubtful encounters
    lead to good fortune, resolute acts,
    happy unions, sires and sons.
    What is your name, asks one of another,
    the tale of our lives constructing itself
    seamlessly,
a thickly woven fabric of eventful threads.
But the spool is empty, it goes on its way,
    talking to itself in an odd singsong,
while the fathers hurry across crowded streets,
    anxious to see if they can yet provide
    for offspring still unborn.

There are beings that can wait patiently forever:
    they will outlive the children
    though they are children themselves,
    neglected innocents newly created,
    creatures granted a purpose
    revealed to be obsolete.
    The machines have come to life—
but even if they were to disassemble themselves,

some unspoken guilt, unrevealed violation,
would send them to the courtyards and damp basements
where remote kinships still survive.

Odradek,
blessed little object,
sinister thing with a storybook past,
the age endures so long as you remain
senseless, upright, heir and inheritance,
while the kids tumble about on the landing
and their parents stare disconsolately
at the form which things assume in oblivion.

A Poem for the Great Heresy

The Demiurge was in love with consummate, superb,
and complicated materials; we shall give priority to
trash. We are simply entranced and enchanted by the
cheapness, shabbiness, and inferiority of material.
—BRUNO SCHULZ

In back rooms
among decades of rubbish,
the moldering ruins of upholstered lives,
the dust turns freely about half-torn labels
bearing the names of ancient firms
long since defunct.

God is a face
pressed against the window panes
of attics, basements, abandoned houses,
where in closets beneath staircases
still may be found
the traces of a secondary, hibernal creation.

Piles of oddments,
random accumulations
of all that is refused its further use,
stir, twitch, test tremulous limbs,
shiver into life.

From provincial gardens given to weeds,
matter pullulates, forgetful of the seasons,
enticed to emulate
divine emanations:
the ectoplasmic furniture of junk.

Imagine the sadness of men transformed
        into rubber tubes, alarm bells,
the gutted insides of clockwork figurines
        whirring forever in a jungle of burs;
as the sky above them emits clouds of birds,
leaking sawdust from the astral geometry,
        the mechanized dome
of some remote, absolute and final firmament.

For Sinai is stitched out of serge and gabardine;
        and the Book of the Law holds the accounts
of dry goods shops, somnolent antiquarians,
        small-town merchants in faded caftans
who blow the shofar above the heads of their customers
        crowded among bolts of cloth.

    Why then does life sputter and collapse,
        leaving the world in elemental boredom
as the gray rash of dusk covers the wallpaper
and the townfolk stroll out on their evening constitutional
        beneath the sign of the Cyclist
        newly raised into the heavens?

    There is no competing with the Demiurge,
    there is no solace in cardboard and feathers;
    and the doomsday palimpsest abruptly inscribed
    upon a single page of the Book of the Year
        reads November 19, 1942.

Homage to Naftali Brandwine

A few are chosen in every generation,
and though it seems the numbers may dwindle,
be unafraid. The twilight deepens into evening,
and the stars, heeding the clarinet,
shake their limbs, upon which are written
all the names of God.

Behind the tenacious myths,
as behind the sweet storm of melody,
is a vacancy that few dare approach.
It holds and fascinates until the notes steal in,
shimmering, changing— Look!
here is the Bronx and not Galicia:
we may as well have ridden the wind.

Janusz Korczak

The banner of the king
who lived in a book
waved above the orphans'
last procession.

Not in myth alone
does murder make for art
nor the death of youth
leave suspect promises.

Be wary of images
bequeathed to history
lest they turn into relics
at local shrines.

Protect the memories
like the winter protects seeds:
oblivion
may be a great god too.

Past and Present

Many of these people are still alive,
though I do not see them often.

On city streets or in lawn chairs,
in bathing suits or fur collars,
they look out across a discontinuous space.

And they are framed by my retrospective will,
as if it were I who had imposed
the boundaries of their lives.

Now the album seems full of strangers,
no matter how beautiful the clothing.

Offering

To those who have grown old in the service of Love,
I offer this poem, in which abides
the violence that rests but does not sleep.
Passion, neither master nor servant,
but sometime companion, keeps to its place,
alert to the signs: shall it inscribe
this parchment, this flesh, what little else
we have to give?

The old turn into stories about themselves,
sing little songs: as they fall asleep,
they seem to fall into deep wells
in which angry waves are gathered and calmed.
Sometimes you are gone, Mother and Father:
I feel protected as much by the words.
To those who have grown old in the service of the poem,
I offer my love.

Prayer

for Steven

Last night I looked at the stars;
The baby lay in my arms.
And as I looked at the stars
Wheeling the planet round,
I knew I could not rest:
I felt as one addressed.

It brought me close to prayer
That such a thing could be.
You know, we think of prayer
As that which must be said:
What had I to say last night
To the stars' abstract light?

A Concert
at the First Unitarian Church
Cincinnati, Ohio
Yom Kippur, 5744
the hundredth birthday of William Carlos Williams

Sharp sword of remembrance, torch of self-knowledge,
key to no door I can open now,
a robed figure whose face I cannot see:
why this pagan vision staring down at me,
reviving my remorseful faith?

At the front of Bellarmine Chapel there is a cross,
hieratic memorial to pain,
and in Beth Shalom, a closet with a book—
but in this alien temple, stand and look—
there is a window, opaque though it may be.

Williams drove along and diagnosed the world:
it was perfect, and perfectly rank.
The grass grew wild, go where he would.
The people idled. He saw that it was good,
sat down and clattered out his pastorals.

I turn from him like every other father.
Words set to music, image stained in glass,
silence: these are what I love.
The stars are not messages inscribed above,
for which knowledge I may yet atone.

Plaint

My somnolent angel
rests on the cornice
of an ancient temple
too long unused.

Her palm beneath her chin,
she gazes across the valley:
no smoke rises,
no birds fly.

Shall Love receive her
when she finally stirs?
The weathered frieze
holds no answer:

all the myths exclude her.
How patiently she waits,
Psyche's little sister,
staring at the dawn.

Mirror

Entangled in the flesh, there are always those
whose grace obscures their lapses and limits,
which become a mirror to our uncertainty.
Our image confronts us on a surface of regret,
however beautiful its frame.

Wedding

Shapely days: grass at the ankles,
pearls or scarves about the waist.
The moment is a wedding, a disenfranchised feast,
from which certain guests remove themselves
as the evening's entertainment proceeds.

Wound

Splendor is a metaphor,
    a wandering meaning
that has come to rest;

a defense against knowledge
    unspoken yet pervasive.

Shall it build itself a throne
    or recede into nothingness?
—as if there were a choice.

You must sacrifice your son
    on the altar of your beauty,
irrevocably veiled
    but still preserved.

And they came with knives,
    slurbs and consonants,
engineered intrusions,
    brittle remains.

So the romance of the ruins
    was projected upon language:
this is the inheritance.

This is the inheritance:
    glebes and lost fortunes
and a voice made of ice

—speaking in the desert.

No ram with his horns
        entangled in a thorn bush;
no one replying
        "Here I am."

Presence and absence
        impressing themselves
upon each other's flesh,
        until pain is a pleasure

beneath a canopy of wings
        which hides the sky.

Drafts and Fragments

Gentile or Jew
O you who turn the wheel and look to windward,
Consider Phlebas, who was once handsome and tall as you.
—T. S. ELIOT,
The Waste Land

Phlebas the Phoenician, bearer of letters,
drowned on his return voyage.
Before his ship went down in the storm
of jealous Modernists seeking revenge,
he had stayed for a while in a sunny harbor town
where he lectured briefly at the local academy.

Phlebas the Phoenician wrote in the sand,
offering certain signs of his qualifications.
He maintained to the last that he was merely a scribe,
despite the obvious novelty of his teachings.
The crocodiles came up out of the river
to bask anachronistically upon the shore,
while Phlebas spoke of the dangers of speculation.

He ate olives and bread, spent time in the wineshop;
the proprietor, seeming to remember him,
lent him a cot in the back room.
One becomes attached to certain anecdotes,
no matter how disreputable their sources.

אֱמֶת

for William Bronk

You are not required to complete the work, but
neither are you free to desist from it.
—RABBI TARPHON

Have I loved the Torah more than God,
sailing in an ark to the homeland of the text:
or have I been recalled by a handful of slogans,
 the leaking resonance of glamorous tropes
  reduced to empty shells?

The primal vowel is caught in the throat:
aleph, the utterance which precedes the truth,
in which is contained the formula of negation,
 mem and *tav:* to be found at last
  inscribed on any forehead.

The clay collapses upon the creator,
 the letters lie in a heap:
or freed from the flesh, do they rise upward,
 seeking the limiting code?

Bound and unbound to the limits of the world:
 covenant prior to all known covenants:
from a displaced source come restless messengers,
 yearning for authority from absent kings.

Four Impromptus

I.

Those who are speaking will go on speaking
as from the mouth of a cave sounds issue forth
continually, unintelligible but portentous,
from which one stands back in awe or fear.
Can mere difficulty be rendered into music?
or does a simple idea multiply itself endlessly,
so that finally one is convinced of the sense of it,
interprets it, speaks likewise. The carpet unravels,
the jigsaw puzzle breaks into bits.

Something has been obscured here,
some figure standing in a recessed space,
cloaked, engaged in mystery.
Throw back the hood: it is you or me,
it is anyone, smiling, and the place,
lit up, now looks more familiar.
Yes, we have been here before,
not merely because we return
like some fond vacationers to a summer cottage,
but because we have learned that any spot
can lend itself to ritual.

This is what comes of a desire for purity—
utter promiscuity, which is not a matter
of morality, but of integrity, keeping things together,
keeping things themselves, even when you know they're not.
Alice remains our mascot: a raging ego
eating, drinking, changing but remaining the same.
One is led down the same corridors,
sets to sea in the same sieve,

falls in love with the same girl
who departs and leaves you playing on your pipe.

Apparently random, such labor proceeds
until a camp is set up on the border of parody,
which is to be found two steps in any direction.
It takes a peculiar heroism (now common property)
to recognize this, a singular gaiety
disguising itself, vacillating with despair.

2.

Now I want to go into that world,
crossing the border, leaving the names
and the places, the constant displays,
knowing a little, perhaps having been
where men sit and hear each other groan.

I want to say yes to this world
although it is a poor simulacrum,
replica of forest, of garden and estate,
all done in papier-mâché. The puppets
with strings that go up to the sky,
their big heads nodding, white hands clapping:
do they live here or do they come and go,
making a home where they can?

It is only in the imagination
that birds are worth following,
that the moon rises like a skull over the ocean,
and the symbols order themselves nicely,
waiting to be observed. And so I have come here
to sleep among the flowers,
where nothing can do me harm.

But before you leave I have to tell you
that I have always loved you, and plan to return.
The engineers are moving the clichés into place
as if to build a wall. How daunting
to live among deliberations
which always adopt the guise of accident,
speeding you away from lofty utterance
while offering the image of a kiss.
The necessary resistance is strained and beautiful,
beautiful because it knows all the strains
and plays them over and over
on its violin.

3.
This is where the goblins come in
and steal the baby
and hide it in a cave.

These are the goblins
who shadowed the old man,
leading him astray
as he walked in the forest.

With feathers in their hair,
with boots and bracelets,
these are the ghosts
who haunted the city.

Sweet servants of anarchy,
why do I love you?
I regret the summer day
when you first appeared to me.

I regret how charming
I found your dances.
I regret your embraces.

Perhaps it was a clearing,
perhaps a playground.
I have forgotten everything
but glasses and scarves.

Is poetry a war
that it should leave these ruins,
these poems, these wounds?
Is poetry a war?

Sickness passes
like a distant horseman,

like horses passing
from day to night.

But I lie in my bed
and the spectres pass before me.
When will they pinch me?
When will they kiss me again?

4.
Reb Derasha opened,
saying that the verse
was nothing but its interpretation,
dissolving into its opposite
and passing away.

Reb Derasha sat
for forty days and forty nights,
reading from the book
that has no ending,
the book of open doors,
the book of moons.

Like a candle at noon
sat Reb Derasha,
until his hands turned silver
and his beard transparent.

The wise men debate
like candles in the dark;
they stay up all night
like lovers in a tower
—but come to no conclusions.

So I gave my love an ultimatum:
be unto me a book
which will remain uninterpretable,
and let your body be bound
so that I might read at will.

And when I awoke,
the letters of the alphabet
were asleep beside me.
My love was gone,

and so I read her absence
in the space she had given me.

Now she sits in the Great Assembly
and debates the scholars.
She entertains the young men.

And sometimes I see a star fall,
and sometimes I hear a cricket.
Here in my cell
I am awake before dawn.

In Switzerland

I am not here to write, but to be mad.
— ROBERT WALSER

You imagine them making their way
down muddy roads or through alpine meadows.
Do they carry sticks? Do little dogs follow them?
The accoutrements of poverty appear almost natural:
        they play upon little flutes
and the music careens among the mountains.

Do not feel ashamed when you find yourself crying;
        but do not envy them:
    your leisure hours, however brief,
impress you with an understanding of time
    more tragic than their confusion
        —or so they whisper to you
    whenever their names are recorded.

By the Wayside

The farmer in his field rests for a moment,
rooted in place.
There is a shadow on the road
heading west toward the city,
turning in upon itself as it makes its way.
These rags, this book of unbound pages:
vulnerable,
as a breeze caresses the plowed earth.

In the Study

How rare and beautiful among the arcana
is this simple truth.

So the work is finished and he sends it off
to a reliable printer, though not without regret.

A Poem for Scholars

They frequently suffered hunger. Hunger leads to
sleeplessness, and night-long insomnia arouses a
desire to delve into the mysteries of Cabala.

—I. L. PERETZ

Here is one whose metaphysical hunger
ranges without limits across the field of the body.
Once he dreamed of uniting with his betrothed;
          now he sleeps no more.
Though they say he yearns for the Torah,
who comes to men like a woman to her lover,
          he casts doubt upon the metaphor
          as he buries his nose in a book.

Some things will not yield to the text;
          they remain beyond the play of words
no matter how often they give themselves to speech:
          God had a Book but created the world,
          yearning for the pleasures of the flesh.

So put down your pen and come to supper:
          rye bread, lentil soup, a glass of wine.
Some say such a life is contingent upon luxury;
          others would disagree.
          Like all old tales,
          this one is careless of its end.

Old Photographs and Tarnished Brass

Somewhere an accordion is playing,
as if he needs a reminder of homely life.
          The music is faint
and he cannot bear the interruptions.

He has heard about the enthusiasms,
the letters swelling disproportionately
before the eyes of amazed multitudes;
          the letters disappearing,
the multitudes remaining amazed.

          Instead the walls are contracting,
as solemnly, a snail withdraws into itself
          upon a trembling leaf.
He could walk in the garden and see it all occur
          or read it in a book.

After the Fall

Because she is mute, nature mourns.
—WALTER BENJAMIN

I went into the garden, and I heard among the trees
a murmuring sound, as a lament:
and as if one could cultivate that sound,
I took it upon myself
to plant in a bed already planted,
and so lay down.

The archaic places twist themselves up
out of new soil, there to rest
upon the belly of the earth: there to be loved;
as given over to desire,
music finds itself resting, or after a long time,
inchoate tears finally fall
from eyes too long held up against the sun.

The flowers thrive in shade so they may die;
and horrible truth walks barefoot,
drinks wine at noon and eats roasted flesh,
prophesies and departs.
—Stay out of the desert, there is madness there!
and the intrusive voice is suddenly a spring
of water, and a quiet return.

I went into the garden, and I saw among the trees
two figures walking hand in hand;
and it was as if nothing had ever changed:
the years are leaves that never fall,
though empty spaces are made out of sound
and lovers hide in closed rooms.

A Poem for the Abyss

The Romantic stood among the things of nature:
the wind was the wind, the clouds were clouds;
the trees shook their branches and the Romantic was tempted
to rush back home to his books.
He could endure so little, tolerate so little,
for whom the things of nature were pages turning,
themes among other themes.

The Romantic believed he had come to worship,
but all he could discover was dread.
When the moon was hidden and the roaring wind
refused to be a metaphor for the human voice,
he was aware of a trembling which included his body,
but extended beyond into nothing he could perceive
and nothing that wanted a name.

How still it was behind the wind:
a handful of stars shone forth in darkness,
and at the base of the tree nothing stirred.
This was what he had hoped for:
a great clearing of the sky,
and a clearing of being, a sounding of the soul.

My Father's Yahrzeit

I wanted to tell you how the light was falling,
as if the whole evening had been lit for you
        not like some crude candle,
    but as a confluence of summer airs
    cooled to a rare degree of comfort
    like a hand upon the forehead
        or a kiss upon the cheek.

I wanted to tell you that lighting a candle
        in no way testifies to the darkness
        which I no longer carry with me,
but have put away in a box of mementoes,
        only rarely to bring to light.

When the sun sets and the trees no longer
glow green and gold and sway in gentle glory,
I want you to know that I have withdrawn into myself
        as you did, once and many times,
when the silence neither wounded nor healed
and the shadows on the lawn lengthened, lengthened,
surrounding the children and luring them away.

When the light goes out and the voice ceases,
        this poem could be an old translation,
           a case of mistaken identity,
        poised precipitously between the past
which we have been fooled into thinking we know
        and the future which misleads us
        into thinking it is always unknown.

Job's Daughters

After the storm subsided and all was restored,
they would walk together down by the river
while their father sat before the door of his house,
    thinking about what had changed
    before dozing off in contentment.

These are the women who had somehow won names
as signs of their father's righteousness.
And as each friend had given Job a gold coin or a ring,
the Unnameable had given them parts in the story.
They would walk among the oxen and the sheep
as if nothing could bring them greater happiness.
And if a man were thirsty they would draw water from the well,
and their smiles would calm his yearning.

"Dove," I said as I walked along with them,
    "Cinnamon and Eye-shadow:
you are equal in wealth to all of your brothers
    and fair beyond all other women.
    In you the Face turns toward us,
    and thus you are beloved."

"No," they answered, "we are only names
in an old legend that has somehow been preserved.
We are only aspects of happiness
who appear when all have been reconciled,
though the questions remain unanswered
and the disputes still haunt the air.
And our story is only the story of an image
of unspecified beauty, unreal fulfillment."

We walked in pairs,
Dove and Cinnamon,
Eye-shadow and I:
peace, abundance, and womanly grace,
their names interpreting the limits of their souls;
the commentator standing inside the text
but forever circumscribed.

And in the evening when I lay down,
who was it that came to me there?
The cries of joy that echoed in the stars
are inscribed in no margins,
cannot be emended,
but underwrite each telling of the tale.

Mládi

You know, sometimes the feeling itself is so
overwhelming and strong that the notes hide under it
and flee.

—JANÁČEK

He sat by the window in the darkness
and thought about the death of love.
The night birds' song provided some comfort,
            but it was never enough
for a man who had spent his whole life waiting
by a door that always seemed about to open.
Far away there were horns that seemed to blend
with the breathing of the others asleep in the house.

            She barely thought about him,
but when she did she knew he was thinking of her
            as she walked briskly past the shop windows
            or listened to the concerts in the park.
            He was thinking about her now,
            a fool in both their eyes,
but somehow his thoughts sounded like a horn
            and she was calling to him to come down.

            At first he hardly recognized himself,
            but when she led him past the church
                  where the boys' choir rehearsed
                  he remembered why he had come.
He had cast off his years like an old suit of clothes,
            slipping past Death as a schoolboy escapes
                  from another tedious class.
And like a scholar in love he had studied his mistress

so that he knew her walk despite her veil
    as he followed close behind.

It was a melodious dream of the previous century,
a provincial dream of fiddles in the marketplace,
        opening on a day like any of the days
            on which he might have been born.
        The inn was almost too homey
    except that the birds kept shifting keys,
            separating and varying the motifs
                in a way that was yet to come.
    Still, there was wine and pork with apples,
    and later her arms, her hair at dusk,
            silencing all the songs.

            Silence? oh, trickster! thief!
    Not love but *Liebestod* was drawing near.
Bring back the distances and let them remain
        real, through which sounds might move.
What else could an old man give her but music?
        something that would break her heart
                or make her glad.

Friday Night in the Garden of Eden

The Emblem

One is alone;
two stand before him;
many are playing for the pleasure of all.

One withdraws;
two split asunder;
many are scattered where there were none.

I.

All the little things that make up this world
    once were charged with a unified power:
    a myth: but that was their power,
their proximity demanding a reciprocal distance.

If I were to tell you how much I loved you,
    a Power would come and stand between us.
    I love you: words struggle and cross the void,
but I always wonder if they finally reach you.

Some few of us still sense the withdrawal,
    aware of it in all of our measures,
    all of our gestures: as if had been set
a flaming sword at all of our gates.

Lawrence painted a watercolor:
    Adam and Eve defeating the angel,
    rushing past him to reclaim Paradise.
I cannot imagine they would have been happy,

knowing what they knew. They knew
      love was an ache, dissatisfaction;
      and all their pleasure now depended
upon an absence at the center of their lives.

2.

The musicians played as if at a wedding
      and the audience appeared to understand.
      But we didn't rise and dance,
and joy passed just above our heads.

The musicians played and we had to be satisfied,
      though the bride failed to make her appearance.
      The badkhan made jokes, and the lonely bridegroom
laughed and shattered the glass without her.

The musicians played, and the world's asymmetry
      persisted. Music is nothing but currents of air
      and nothing is ever mended.
Still, the musicians played.

3.

On Friday night in the Garden of Eden,
      Ha-Shem is listening to music,
      which is to say he is creating it
and the angels all join in.

Below, as Milton tells us,
      Adam instructs Eve about the night:
      celestial voices join in cloudy bands
while Satan lurks, invisible reproach.

Music is love, and this is the primal scene
   as well as that other to which we return.
   Long before Adam imparadis't Eve,
Ha-Shem wooed the Shekinah with sound and light

which could not be contained.
   Because we were not content with myths,
   we fell: the myths were fulfilled,
becoming myths. Tell them over and over,

for they yield a certain music, nothing more.

Sketch for a Portrait

As a young man he sat in cafés,
his talents affirmed by the cognoscenti.
How eagerly they awaited his second novel,
since republished in a poor translation.

No elegant patron provided a villa,
and rumors of love affairs have proven false:
he lived alone on a small income
in a run-down suburb of the provincial capital.

Some remember his gestures,
which were at times extravagant;
and some remember a winter evening,
informally hosted and sparsely attended.

He dropped out of sight soon after,
sailing perhaps from Turkey
or a port on the Black Sea.

Braids

Lost in Lindisfarne plaited lines
—BASIL BUNTING

There are words
that bind meanings to themselves
as if they were the strands of a great braid
forever being wound.
"Turn it and turn it again,
for everything is in it":
the words are infinitely interpretable,
the commentaries too numerous to count.
But all of them provide sustenance
as do these braided loaves of bread,
glazed and crowned with poppy seeds,
the patterns almost legible,
scattered as the bread is sliced.

And Samuel slept in the high priest's house,
waking one night to the sound of a voice
urgently calling his name.
Such were the terms of that mysterious election:
he was taken from his parents,
summoned to do the bidding of an alien god:
that is, he was taught to speak.

All things called into being
share in this one quality:
as they were spoken, so do they speak;
the world perceived as a texture of sound,
revealed fold upon fold.
The days too form nodes of meaning:

strands of time come bearing events,
weaving themselves into elaborate coincidences
until the past is gathered into a single moment,
                waiting to be understood.
                But it is never complete,
                never to be finished,
and history proves as inadequate as biography
                as a telling of the tale.
                None of this is meaningful;
it hovers in the void that precedes utterance,
bearing within it a multitude of lights
                waiting to be lit.

The candle is burning;
                its three wicks are formed
                        in the light of a single flame.
The Shekinah uncoils her braids
                and her hair covers the page.
The Sabbath of memory is over:
                an invisible hand unbinds the past
                and the words fall away.

The Contemporary Poetry Series

EDITED BY PAUL ZIMMER

The Contemporary Poetry Series

EDITED BY BIN RAMKE

Norman Finkelstein is a professor of English at Xavier University. He is the author of *The Utopian Moment in Contemporary American Poetry*. His poems have appeared in numerous publications, including *Salmagundi, Denver Quarterly, Missouri Review*, and *Shofar*.